Contents

Spring Phoned

Yesterday
spring phoned to say
it was on its way.

It left
a chirpy message
on nature's answering machine.

And as I lie in bed today
I hear the birds playing the message
over and over again.

Ian Souter

Poems
about
Seasons

Chosen by Brian Moses
Illustrated by Ellie Jenkins

WAYLAND
www.waylandbooks.co.uk

First published in Great Britain in 2015 by Wayland
Copyright © Wayland, 2015

Editor: Victoria Brooker
Designer: Lisa Peacock

ISBN: 978 0 7502 9181 1
Library eBook ISBN: 978 0 7502 9182 8

10 9 8 7 6 5 4 3 2 1

Wayland, an imprint of Hachette Children's Group
Part of Hodder & Stoughton
Carmelite House
50 Victoria Embankment
London EC4Y 0DZ

An Hachette UK Company
www.hachette.co.uk
www.hachettechildrens.co.uk

Printed and bound in China

Acknowledgements:
The Compiler and Publisher would like to thank
the authors for allowing their poems to appear in
this anthology. of poems. Poems © the authors.
While every attempt has been made to gain permissions
and provide an up-to-date biography, in some cases
this has not been possible and we apologise for any
omissions. Should there be any inadvertent omission,
please apply to the Publisher for rectification.

'Snow Joke' was first published in 'Funny Poems for
Christmas' compiled by Paul Cookson (Scholastic
2006)

All websites were valid at the time of going to press.
However, it is possible that some addresses may have
changed to closed down since publication. While the
Publisher and Compiler regret any inconvenience this
may cause the readers, no responsiblity for any such
changes can be accepted by either the Compiler or the
Publisher.

SPRING

Spring's the time for daffodils
And catkins flippy-floppy,
Woolly lambs and fluffy chicks,
And rabbits hippy-hoppy.

Spring's the time for sunny days,
When sparrows flitter-flutter,
Splishy-splashy rainy days
And puddles in the gutter.

Clare Bevan

Springtime
in Bluebell Wood

A million leaves
on trees so tall.
You'll hear birds sing
and cuckoos call
     in Bluebell Wood.

See butterflies,
hear pigeons coo.
The long grass is
still wet with dew
     in Bluebell Wood.

Look! Ferns unfurl,
and green frogs leap.
Brown rabbits hop
and beetles creep
    in Bluebell Wood.

A stile to climb.
A sunny day.
Just stand and watch
the bluebells sway
    in Bluebell Wood.

Wes Magee

Spring in the City

Spring has come to the city,
to the streets and the railway line.
Winter is packing its bags,
the sun has begun to shine.

The cherry tree in our garden
wears a wedding dress of white.
Geese are in flight once more
and days are warm with delight.

There are plenty of baby lambs
to see at the city farm,
and a single primrose shows its head
at the dump, like a lucky charm.

8

A heron is raising its young
at the flooded gravel pits,
and the nest box on our garden wall
is a shelter for baby tits.

Wrens are finding new homes
in an untidy, overgrown hedge.
Pigeons choose a tall building
and jostle for space on a ledge.

Spring has come to the city,
there's a lightness in everyone's tread.
Office workers have shed their coats,
there's a promise of summer ahead.

Brian Moses

What is Summer For?

Summer is for sunhats,
for sandals or bare feet.
Summer is for sunshades,
to shelter from the heat.

Summer is for picnics
and playing in the park.
Summer is for staying out
all day long till dark!

Kate Williams

Summer Clouds

Clouds are drifts of soft white flowers
strewn across a placid blue lake.

Clouds are slow white jellyfish
floating in a clear blue ocean.

Clouds are angry black panthers
crouched, snarling, over the hills.

Clouds are thundering black horses
rearing and tossing their stormy heads.

Penny Kent

Bed in Summer

In winter I get up at night
And dress by yellow candle-light.
In summer, quite the other way,
I have to go to bed by day.

I have to go to bed and see
The birds still hopping on the tree,
Or hear the grown-up people's feet
Still going past me in the street.

And does it not seem hard to you,
When all the sky is clear and blue,
And I should like so much to play,
To have to go to bed by day?

R. L. Stevenson

13

Dear Summer

Dear Summer, you're always my favourite.
I really do like you a lot.
You come every year,
and I'm glad when you're here.
I don't even mind that you're hot.

Dear Summer, whenever you visit,
I love to go outside to play.
I get to wear shorts
and play summertime sports,
or sometimes do nothing all day.

I put on my goggles and swim suit,
and head for the beach or the park.
I go for a hike
or I ride on my bike,
and stay awake long after dark.

Dear Summer, I'm glad you could join us.
Without you, it won't be the same.
I promise I know
that you do have to go,
but, still, it seems sort of a shame.

I'm sure that I'm going to miss you.
The school year is finally here.
I had so much fun
playing out in the sun.
I guess that I'll see you next year.

Kenn Nesbitt

The Swallow

Fly away, fly away, over the sea,
 Sun-loving swallow, for summer is done.
Come again, come again, come back to me,
 Bringing the summer and bringing the sun.

Christina Rossetti

Autumn?

Some people call it 'Autumn'
Some people call it 'Fall'
I call it 'Damp Dark Squelch Time'
As I don't like it at all.

Chris White

Autumn Song

There's a chill in the air
that wasn't there
just over a month ago.

There's a dew on the grass
each morning I pass
the field where the stream runs slow.

People gathering hops,
farmers harvesting crops,
the countryside all of a bustle:

the stubble is burning,
the tractors are churning
and at night the leaves eerily rustle.

Ripe apples are falling,
lonely church bells are calling,
over orchards they sullenly ring.

The summer plants wilt
and my bed gets a quilt,
how I wish I could sleep until spring.

John Rice

Autumn Action Rhyme

Here are the trees
so leafy and tall.

(Stand with arms up as branches,

hands and fingers extended)

Look at the leaves
as they shrivel and fall.

(Curl up hands, then use them to show

leaves falling down toward ground)

Listen and hear
what a whispery sound

(Place hand up to ear to suggest listening.

Some children can make whispery noises too.)

they make as they flutter
and float to the ground.

(Bring leaf-hands right down to rest on

floor for brief pause.)

Here are the branches,
so naked and plain.

(Stand and extend arms again, this time with

fists closed and arms slightly drawn in.)

waiting for Spring
when the leaves grow again.

(Open hands to show fingers stretching out.

Push arms out a little to emphasise gesture.)

Tony Mitton

Sounds Like the Winter

Winter is CRUNCH!
Snow underfoot
Winter is SNIP!
Wrapping paper is cut
Winter is WHOOSH!
Cold winds blow
Winter is GIGGLE!
Play in the snow
Winter is LA LAAAA!
Carol-singing group
Winter is SLURP!
Drinking hot soup
Winter is MMMMMM!
Give the pudding a stir
But above all else
Winter is BRRRRRRRRRRRRR!

Chris White

I Hear Thunder

I hear thunder, I hear thunder.
    (Stamp feet on floor.)
Hark, don't you? Hark, don't you?
    (Put hand to ear.)
Pitter-patter raindrops,
    (Move hand down slowly, waggling fingers.)
Pitter-patter raindrops,
I'm wet through –
    (Shake body.)
You are too.
    (Point to someone else.)

Anon

December

December, December,
A month to remember,
A month full of darkness and light,
A month full of rushing
And sharing and hoping.
A month full of one special night.

Daphne Kitching

Mr Snowman

Monday built our Snowman
Sitting proud and fat
Tuesday gave him a football scarf
And the warmest woolly hat
Wednesday gave him his button eyes
Thursday a carrot nose
Friday gave him sticks for arms
And Saturday more clothes
But Sunday gave bad weather
The sky began to cry
Sunday took our snowman
We never said goodbye.

Debra Bertulis

Snow Joke

Why does it have to be Snowmen?
Why is it never Snowgirls?
Why can't we build a Snow-Princess
With berries for rubies and pearls?
Why can't we pick her some holly
And give her a spiky, green crown?
What about icicle diamonds
To wear on her glittery gown?
What about crowds of Snow Ladies
With twiggy and twizzly curls?
Why does it have to be Snowmen?
Why is it NEVER Snowgirls?

Clare Bevan

The Seasons in Me

I can be sunny,
I can be warm,
I can blow hot and cold,
I can thunder and storm.

I can be breezy,
I can be bright.
I can be dark
I can be light.

I can be wet,
I can be dry,
I can change like the seasons
in the blink of an eye.

From the outside
can anyone see
that inside I have
all the seasons in me?

Jane Clarke

Time

Seconds to minutes
And hours into days;
The gleam of the Moon
And the Sun's golden rays;
Through weeks, months and years
The clocks tick and chime
As they show, the World over,
The passing of Time!

Dandelions; sun dials;
The clock in the hall;
A wrist-watch; Big Ben;
Clocks great and clocks small.
They all show how Time
Is unwilling to stay –
And how quickly Tomorrow
Turns into Today!

Trevor Harvey

Further information

Once a poem in this book has been read, either individually, in groups or by the teacher, check with the children that they have understood what the poem is about. Ask them to point out any difficult lines or words and explain these. Ask the children how they feel about the poem. Do they like it? Is there a certain section or line of the poem that they particularly enjoy?

After reading Ian Souter's poem 'Spring Phoned', children could consider what messages other seasons might leave on nature's answer machine. Maybe autumn's message would be the honking of geese as they migrated south for the winter.

'Spring' by Clare Bevan lists a lot of the things we associate with spring. Maybe something similar could be written for the other seasons. Children can pick out the rhyming words in Wes Magee's 'Spring in Bluebell Wood'. Both this poem and 'Spring in the City' by Brian Moses are observation poems. Children could visit a local wood or a town to observe signs of spring for themselves. Such collections of observations could be used in children's own writing.

'What is Summer For?' by Kate Williams is a useful model poem for children's own poetry. Other seasons can be written about using a repeating pattern of "Autumn is..." or "Winter is...". Look at the metaphors in Penny Kent's 'Summer Clouds' – why do they look like "slow white jellyfish?" Children can come up with their own ideas by looking at clouds themselves.

'Bed in Summer' by R.L. Stevenson is something that all children should be familiar with. 'Dear Summer' by Kenn Nesbitt would work well as a performance poem for 5 voices. The rhyming pattern is a little different here. Can children pick this out? Maybe children could write letters to other seasons.

'Autumn Song' by John Rice uses yet another rhyming pattern which the children can identify. Poems from the book can be compared and the children can decide which way of rhyming appeals to them most.

Children may wish to learn 'Autumn Action Rhyme' by Tony Mitton and perform it to other children. They could add sound effects including shakers and scrapers, or home-made instruments – crackly crisp packets, autumn leaves in a bag and so on. Chris White's 'Sounds Like Winter' is again a poem that can be used as a model for writing about other seasons and the sounds we associate with them, again adding sound effects.

'Mr Snowman' by Debra Bertulis, could be written in another form, maybe the snowman writing his diary for the week. Clare Bevan's 'Snow Joke' might make children think about why we always say gingerbread man, or stick man. Can they think of other examples?

Children can write their own versions of 'The Seasons in Me' by Jane Clarke, trying to discover different weather words to the ones that she has used. 'Time' by Trevor Harvey would be a good introduction to any project about time, what we think about time passing and how we measure it.

Encourage children to look for further examples of poems about seasons. These can be copied out and then illustrated. Build up a collection of poems and let children talk about their favourites. Let them practise reading and performing the poems adding actions and percussion accompaniment if appropriate.

About the Poets

Debra Bertulis' life-long passion is the written and spoken word, and she is the author of many published poems for children. She is regularly invited into schools where her workshops inspire pupils to compose and perform their own poetry. Debra lives in Herefordshire where she enjoys walking the nearby Welsh hills and seeking out second-hand book shops!
www.debrabertulis.com

Clare Bevan used to be a teacher until she decided to become a writer instead. So far, she has written stories, plays, song lyrics, picture books and a huge heap of poetry. Her poems have appeared in over one hundred anthologies, and she loves performing them in schools. Her hobbies are reading and acting, and she once dressed up as a farmyard chicken.

Jane Clarke is the author of over 80 children's books including the award-winning picture books *Stuck in the Mud*, illustrated by Gary Parsons, and *Gilbert the Great*, illustrated by Charles Fuge. She's delighted to have a poem in this anthology.
www.jane-clarke.co.uk

Trevor Harvey's humorous poems for children have now been included in around 200 anthologies and publications. He has also written one-act plays for amateur dramatic groups (published by Jasper) and has been a judge of play competitions for The Sussex Playwrights' Club and for New Writing South.
www.writersunlimited.co.uk/trevor-harvey

Daphne Kitching lives in East Yorkshire with her husband. She is a former primary school teacher and specialist teacher of pupils with SpLD (Dyslexia), a poet, a pyrographer and a priest in a lively East Riding parish. She loves ladybirds, long walks, learning to knit and keeping up with all her children and grandchildren.

Wes Magee: *Deep in the Green Wood* and *Here come the Creatures* are two of Wes Magee's recent books for children. He lives in a tiny village on the Yorkshire Wolds and has a pet dog, a golden retriever called Maya.

Tony Mitton has been published as a poet for children since the early 90s. He has also written many successful verse picture books and works blending poetry with narrative. He has won several awards. He lives in Cambridge where he continues to read and write. www.tonymitton.co.uk

Brian Moses lives in Burwash in Sussex where the famous writer Rudyard Kipling once lived. He travels the country performing his poetry and percussion show in schools, libraries and theatres. He has published over 200 books including the series of picture books *Dinosaurs Have Feelings Too* for Wayland. www.brianmoses.co.uk

Kenn Nesbitt is an American children's poet. In 2013, he was named Children's Poet Laureate by the Poetry Foundation. He has written many books, including *When the Teacher Isn't Looking and Other Funny Poems About School*, and *The Biggest Burp Ever: Funny Poems for Kids.*

John Rice has published seven collections of poetry for children and his poems have appeared in over 300 anthologies, magazines and newspapers. Several of his poems have been broadcast by the BBC, and some have been set to music. He was Glasgow's Poet-in-Residence for two years during the Robert Burns 250th anniversary celebrations. He lives in Cumbria and regularly visits schools in the north of England and southern Scotland.

Christina Rossetti (1830–94) was an English poet who published a number of books and rhymes for young children, including *Sing Song* and 'Goblin Market' – a fairy story in verse.

Ian Souter is retired from teaching and loves to exercise, play music and travel. He lives in the wilds of Surrey but also loves to visit, in particular, France and Australia. On his travels he also keeps an eye (and an ear) open for words and ideas. Sometimes he finds them hanging from trees or people's mouths or even sparkling in the sunshine.

R.L. Stevenson (1850–94) was a Scottish author and poet. His best-known books are *Treasure Island* and *Kidnapped.* A collection of his poetry – *A Child's Garden of Verses* – is a classic of children's poetry.

Chris White has written many poetry books, including *Don't Put Dave in the Microwave!* and a book of stories including 'Stumpy's Big Adventure.' He illustrates his own work and other writers', too. Chris has taken his poetry performances around the world to places such as China, Dubai and Congo! www.veggievampire.com

Kate Williams When Kate's children were young, she made up poems to read them at bedtime. It was their clever idea that she send them off to a publisher, and she's been contributing to children's anthologies ever since! Kate finds writing a poem is like making a collage, but less sticky – except that she's stuck in the craze! She provides workshops for schools, too. www.poemsforfun.wordpress.com

Index of first lines

Titles in the series:

Poems About Festivals:
978 0 7502 9184 2

Let's Celebrate by Sue Hardy-Dawson
The Chinese Dragon by Catherine Benson
Pancake Day by Debra Bertulis
Holi, Festival of Colour by Punitha Perinparaja
Mother's Day by Eric Finney
Children's Day by Penny Kent
Eid-ul-Fitr by Penny Kent
It's Diwali Tonight by John Foster
Harvest Thanks by Jan Dean
A Hallowe'en Pumpkin by Dorothy Aldis
Fireworks by Judith Nicholls
Eight Candles Burning by Celia Warren
Long, Long Ago
Christmas Eve by Brian Moses
Happy New Year by Brenda Williams

Poems About Seasons:
978 0 7502 9181 1

Spring Phoned by Ian Souter
Spring by Clare Bevan
Springtime in Bluebell Wood by Wes Magee
Spring in the City by Brian Moses
What is Summer For? by Kate Williams
Summer Clouds by Penny Kent
Bed in Summer by R.L. Stevenson
Dear Summer by Kenn Nesbitt
The Swallow by Christina Rossetti
Autumn? by Chris White
Autumn Song by John Rice
Autumn Action Rhyme by Tony Mitton
Sounds Like Winter by Chris White
I Hear Thunder
December by Daphne Kitching
Mr Snowman by Debra Bertulis
Snow Joke by Clare Bevan
The Seasons in Me by Jane Clarke
Time by Trevor Harvey

Poems About Animals:
978 0 7502 9178 1

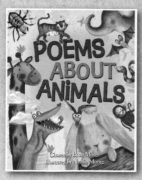

The Terrible Ten by James Carter
On My Way From School by Roger Stevens
Animal Riddles by Marian Swinger
My Dog by Joshua Seigal
Sad Rabbit by Eric Finney
A Bear in his Underwear by Brian Moses
Komodo Dragon by Graham Denton
I'm a Giraffe by Mike Jubb
Hungry Crocodile by Carol Rumble
If You Should Meet a Crocodile
How to Spot a Kangaroo by Robert Scotallero
Caterpillar by Christina Rossetti
Swish Swash by Bill Condon
Tiger by Alison Chisholm
Animal Farewells by Kate Snow

Poems About the Seaside:
978 0 7502 9175 0

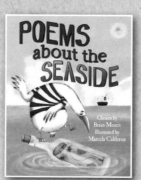

Are We Nearly There Yet? by Brian Moses
Beach Counting by Tony Mitton
I Do Like to be Beside the Seaside by John A. Glover-Kind
The Seagull's Song by June Crebbin
Seagulls With Everything by Brian Moses
Seaside Sounds by John Foster
A Single Wave by Ian Souter
The 7th Wave by Jan Dean
There's an Ocean in This Seashell by Graham Denton
Shells by Debra Bertulis
Skimming Stones on the Sea by Jane Clarke
Treasure Chest Mystery by Kate Williams
Playtime Pirate (Action Rhyme) by Tony Mitton
Letters in Bottles by Clare Bevan
The Bucket by James Carter
Rock Pool by Matt Goodfellow
The Friendly Octopus by Mike Jubb
Crab by Irene Assiba D'Almeida
Man on the Beach by Joshua Seigal